TABLE OF CONTENTS

The RESET WORKBOOK

A FUN, INTERACTIVE WORKBOOK DESIGNED TO HELP YOU USE YOUR CREATIVE VISION TO FIND DAILY BALANCE

QUARTERLY REVIEW

The average person makes about 35,000 decisions on any given day. What do I wear? Where do I park? What should I cook for dinner?

This usually means that by the time you get home from work, you're more likely to veg out in front of the TV than to invest time in making your dreams a reality.

That's why it's vital to take some time to check in with yourself every three months. Pairing your passions with a strategic focus is the easiest way to ensure that your life stays in alignment.

The following section will ask you big and small questions to help inform you when making the best decisions to build your ideal life.

HOW DOES THIS WORK?

Between busy work days and demanding social lives, many of us don't make the time to check in on our goals. We need an easy way to stay accountable.

I've developed a process that is surprisingly straightforward for making a plan to get what you want. It's also pretty fun.

The Reset Workbook is a 90-day planner strategically designed to help you physically interact with your goals. It offers lots of personal analysis, brainstorming opportunities, and inspirational quotes. The primary goal, however, is to build tactical roadmaps to make your dreams a reality.

You answer questions. Brainstorm potential goals. Narrow them down and set intentions for the next three months.

This is a living document meant to be examined regularly and altered to fit your ever-changing version of a fulfilling, meaningful life.

The workbook is separated into specific categories to help you navigate the most vital parts of your personal identity. You'll learn more about yourself and have the tools to design a path that makes you happier and healthier.

There are a few ways you can work through this book.

You can set aside the first hour of your day to review the pages. It will take you between two and four weeks to finish it.

Alternatively, you can take a weekend retreat alone or with a small group of trusted friends and power through the questions.

Either way, The Reset Workbook will pull and stretch you in magical ways.

Write, color, scribble, but most importantly, enjoy!

This book is developed by a real human being—equal parts creative and socially awkward. You can follow me on all your favorite social channels, including Instagram, Facebook, and Twitter at @justinmadethat.

THE BACKSTORY

It all started in 2016—the most difficult year of my life. There was the election. A breakup. And the general malaise of living in an apartment filled with too many memories.

I worked for myself, ran a small design studio, and finally built a successful revenue model.

Yet I felt stuck. I made plenty of money, but I was having trouble finding a work/life balance. My life was so out of sync that I was desperate for a massive change.

So, I started reading books, taking courses, and listening to every podcast on self-help, hoping to find the guidance I needed to redesign my life.

It was a difficult season, but it was also a beautiful moment of personal clarity.

For too many years, I just let life happen to me.

It took months of writing and reading and awkward conversations until I finally took action.

I found the courage to plot out what I wanted to do with my life.

I bought a three-ring binder and decided to explicitly plan the steps necessary to define the Justin I wanted to be. This was the first iteration of The Reset Workbook.

Five years later, my life has transformed. I moved to a new city and did the necessary work to increase my income and pay off debt. I have healthier relationships, a full-time job that I enjoy, and I'm taking care of my body in ways that I never have before.

Let's be clear: My life is not perfect.

There are awesome moments and not-so-awesome moments. But I designed this life, and on those days when I feel uninspired, I am empowered to continue to adapt, grow, and change.

That's actually the beauty of The Reset Workbook. Every time I sense that it's time for a meaningful life change, I can work through the book again and make baby steps for resetting my life again and again.

TOP FIVE MOMENTS

What beautiful things happened in the last three months that exceeded my expectations?

01

02

03

04

05

ALWAYS CHANGING

ONE THING I LEARNED ABOUT MYSELF OVER THE PAST THREE MONTHS:

I'M HAPPY BECAUSE THIS HAPPENED:

THIS QUARTER LED ME TO:

I'M HAPPY THIS ENDED IN THE PAST THREE MONTHS:

USEFUL ADVICE

If I could go back in time, what advice would I give myself?

01

02

03

04

05

06

07

08

09

10

EVERY MOMENT
IS AS PRECIOUS
AS YOU MAKE IT

THINGS THAT ENERGIZE ME

01

02

03

04

05

SO THANKFUL

What is a list of 10 things I'm thankful for, including people, moments, experiences, and things?

01

02

03

04

05

06

07

08

09

10

THINGS THAT MAKE ME FEEL EXHAUSTED

01

02

03

04

05

WANTS

What is a list of things that I want to add to my life right now?

01

02

03

04

05

MIND

The human brain is a beautiful thing. But for many, it can also be a breeding ground for negative thoughts.

Three pounds. 100 billion neurons. The capability of generating 23 watts of power.

While you can't control all of your circumstances, you can always control how you respond to a situation. It all starts with your thoughts.

Your mind is your most valuable resource, and its the primary thing that gives you the confidence and power to succeed.

In this section, we'll focus on the best ways to guard your thoughts and consistently fill your brain with the loving-kindness it deserves.

WHAT'S HOLDING ME BACK?

NAME THE FEAR	HOW CAN I CONQUER THE FEAR?

WHERE IN YOUR LIFE CAN YOU BE MORE COURAGEOUS?

PROFESSIONAL GIFTS

01

02

03

04

05

PERSONAL GIFTS

01

02

03

04

05

MY WEAKNESSES

01

02

03

04

05

06

07

08

09

10

DESCRIBING MYSELF

What are the five adjectives that describe the best version of me?

01

02

03

04

05

DEFINING ME

WHAT IS THE TITLE OF THIS NEXT CHAPTER IN MY LIFE?

WHAT DO I WISH I HAD MORE TIME TO DO?

WHEN DO I FEEL THE MOST LIKE MYSELF?

WHAT IS SOMETHING I LOVE LEARNING ABOUT?

PURPOSE

There's no manual to life, but there are some indisputable truths.

You have a unique set of gifts.

And it is your responsibility to cultivate those gifts and share them because the world desperately needs the uncommon magic you were born to create.

That's the heart of your purpose.

Your gifts: What you want to do?

Your passions: Who do you want to help?

Your values: What magic will you create?

It's a big-picture conceptual idea, but the end result is usually simple.

EXAMPLES OF A PURPOSE STATEMENTS

- My purpose is to use my problem-solving skills to make a significant change in the world.

- My purpose is to bring joy everywhere I go.

- My purpose is to facilitate meaningful connections between the people I encounter.

- My purpose is to pour as much love as I can into the world.

- My purpose is to expose as many parents as possible to the power of therapy for kids.

- My purpose is to make ideas happen.

- My purpose in life is to write stories about the Latinx experience that connect with people's hearts and minds.

- My purpose is to encourage other women to have the courage to start their own businesses.

- My purpose in this season is to create art consistently.

- My purpose is to be a source of peace for everyone I encounter.

- My purpose is to defend the rights of all people and create equality in my workplace.

- My purpose is to give my children a safe and loving home and set them up for future success.

- My purpose in this season is to live life to the fullest and continually have new experiences.

FIND YOUR PURPOSE

We're all here for a specific reason. What are four idea for what my purpose can be?

01

02

03

04

BODY

Your body is your connection to the world.

It's a vessel that holds your marvelous, interesting spirit.

Your body is something to love and cherish.

But for so many of us, our bodies hold so much insecurity and shame.

This section is dedicated to thinking positively about your body and specifically giving you a space to celebrate the beauty you carry with you every day.

Remember: It's important to use positive words that are affirming. In this section, be kind to yourself.

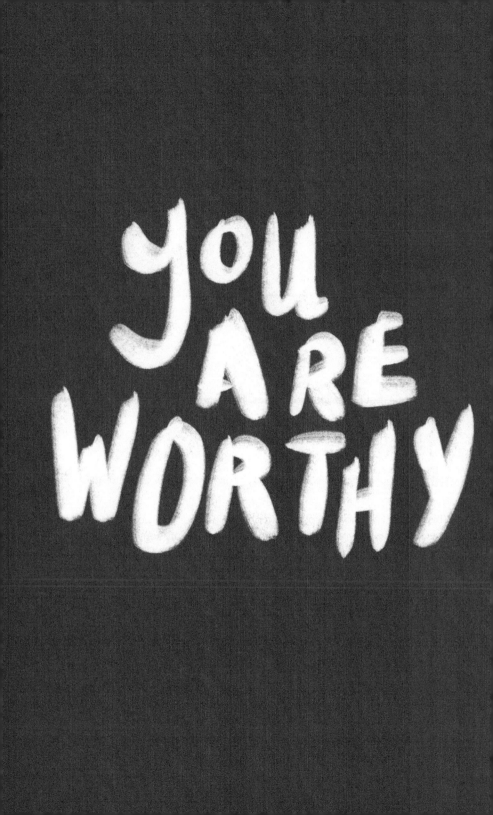

LOVING MY BODY

WHAT DO I LOVE ABOUT MY BODY?

HOW CAN I CONNECT MORE WITH MOTHER NATURE?

WHAT'S SOMETHING THAT MADE ME FEEL BEAUTIFUL IN THE LAST THREE MONTHS?

CONSCIOUSLY CONSUMING

WHAT FOOD MAKES ME FEEL THE MOST ENERGIZED?

HOW CONSCIOUS AM I WHEN I EAT?

WHAT'S MY GO-TO FEEL-GOOD MEAL?

WHAT WOULD I LIKE TO PRIORITIZE EATING IN THE NEXT THREE MONTHS?

LOVING WHAT I SEE

WHAT DO I LOVE ABOUT MY BODY?

ON A SCALE FROM 1-10, HOW GOOD IS MY SLEEP?

HOW DO I RELAX?

HOW WILL I KEEP MY BODY IN MOTION THIS QUARTER?

YOU ALWAYS HAVE A CHOICE

DISCOVERING ME

WHAT'S MY FAVORITE PART OF MY BODY?

HAS MY BODY IMAGE EVER STOPPED ME FROM DOING SOMETHING? HOW CAN I CHANGE THAT?

ON A SCALE FROM 1-10, HOW ACTIVE AM I? WHY IS THAT?

WHAT WOULD THE WORLD LOOK LIKE IF NO ONE HAD LOW BODY CONFIDENCE?

ACCEPTING MY BODY

WHAT DOES BODY ACCEPTANCE MEAN TO ME?

WHEN I THINK OF MY BODY, WHAT'S THE FIRST WORD THAT COMES TO MIND? WHY?

WHEN I THINK OF MY BODY, I'D LIKE TO THINK...

HERE'S A LIST OF REASONS WHY I'M GRATEFUL FOR MY BODY AS IT IS...

I AM BEAUTIFUL

RIGHT NOW, MY BODY NEEDS...

TO ME, A BEAUTIFUL PERSON MUST BE...

WHAT WAS A TIME WHEN I GENUINELY LOVED MY BODY?

I FEEL MOST ATTRACTIVE WHEN...

FOLLOW THE PEACE, RELEASE THE NEGATIVITY

SPIRIT

If your mind is the melody, then your spirit is the bass line.

We often think of our minds and spirits as separate entities. There's overlap for sure, but our minds are constantly changing, while our spirits have a consistent throughline.

That's why it's so valuable to invest time in cultivating your heart.

This section is designed to check in on your spirit and take steps to sustain continued spiritual growth.

Regardless of your background, the idea is to give yourself the space to think outside the body and go deeper into universal truths. This can take a variety of forms: philosophy, religion, or a deep love of nature.

EMOTIONAL RELEASE

Who or what makes me the most angry? What do I need to tell them?

01

02

03

04

TRANSFORMATION
IS ALWAYS
POSSIBLE

HOW'S MY HEART?

HOW MUCH POWER DO DAILY CIRCUMSTANCES HAVE OVER ME? HOW DO I NORMALLY RESPOND TO INCONVENIENCES?

HOW DO I WANT TO BE REMEMBERED?

WHAT DOES LOVE MEAN TO ME?

HOW DO I WANT TO EXPLORE MY CONNECTION TO THE UNIVERSE IN THE NEXT THREE MONTHS?

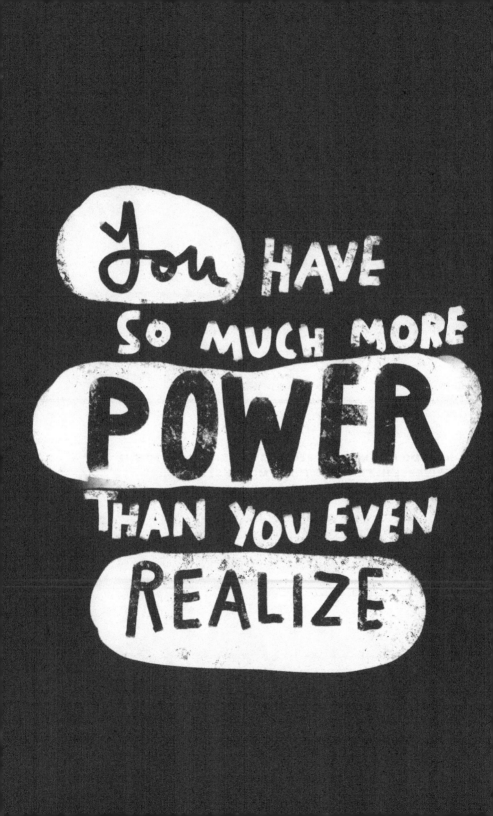

QUOTABLE

There are moments where things won't go my way—moments where I feel totally unmotivated. Here are my favorite quotes for future inspiration.

01

02

03

04

SHARE THE LIGHT

Who are four people who have brought me joy in the last three month?
Write a short message of love to them.

01

02

03

04

NEW AWAKENING

DO I SEEK SOCIAL APPROVAL FROM OTHERS? WHY?

HOW OFTEN DO YOU LOSE MY TEMPER?

ON A SCALE FROM 1-10, HOW WOULD I RATE MY PERSONAL
RELATIONSHIPS?

WORK

The average full-time worker clocks in about 2,087 hours per year, according to the U.S. Office of Personnel Management.

And now more than ever, many people are balancing a full-time job with at least some sort of part-time side hustle to make ends meet.

You deserve to find a career you enjoy 80 percent of the time. But for most people, that career will not be your passion.

Instead, your career will be something that pays you a livable wage that you're passionate about doing well. If you're lucky, it will also afford you the time to explore your interests outside of work.

The purpose of this section is not to get you to quit your day job. It's to help you focus on finding a career that offers a work/life balance.

MY CAREER NEEDS

What are non-negotiable needs I expect from work?

01

02

03

04

05

06

07

08

09

10

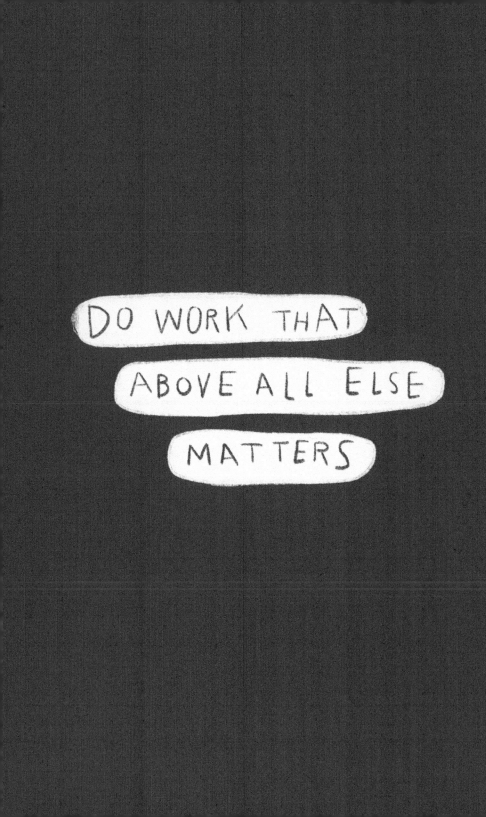

WORK HAPPY

WHAT'S A JOB I'D ABSOLUTELY NEVER WANT TO DO AGAIN?

WHY AM I DOING MY CURRENT JOB?

IF MONEY WEREN'T AN ISSUE, WHAT WOULD I DO WITH MY TIME?

CAREER GOALS

ON A SCALE FROM 1-10, HOW WOULD I RATE THE PAST THREE MONTHS OF MY JOB? WHY?

WHAT DO I LOVE ABOUT MY CURRENT JOB?

WHAT DO I HATE ABOUT MY CURRENT JOB?

IF I COULD HAVE ANY OTHER JOB, WHAT WOULD IT BE?

MY ROLE MODELS

Who are three people I look to for career inspiration?

_____

01

_____

02

_____

03

_____

THE PEOPLE WE ADMIRE REMIND US TO LIVE OUT LOUD

MY WORKING STYLE

WHAT DOES GOING ABOVE AND BEYOND AT WORK MEAN TO ME?

WHAT'S ONE SOLVABLE PROBLEM AT WORK I'D LIKE TO PERSONALLY TACKLE?

ON A SCALE FROM 1-10, HOW GOOD AM I AT TAKING
VACATIONS? WHEN CAN I SCHEDULE SOME TIME OFF?

WHAT COULD I DO A BETTER JOB COMPLETING AT WORK?

THE ONLY PERSON
YOU'RE COMPETING
WITH IS YOUR
PAST SELF

PICTURE OF SUCCESS

WHAT'S ONE LESSON I LEARNED FROM WORK IN THE PAST THREE MONTHS?

WHO'S MY FAVORITE PERSON AT WORK? WHY DO I LIKE THEM SO MUCH?

WHO DO I ADMIRE AT WORK? WHAT QUALITIES FROM THEM WOULD I LIKE TO CULTIVATE IN MYSELF?

IDEAL WORKDAY

Here's my ideal workday, hour by hour.

TIME	ACTIVITY

LOOKING TO MY FUTURE

WHAT'S A PROFESSIONAL ACCOMPLISHMENT OF MINE FROM THE LAST THREE MONTHS?

WHAT DO I WANT MY CAREER TO LOOK LIKE IN THE NEXT FIVE YEARS?

AM I PROFESSIONALLY FULFILLED?

LIFE

It's far too easy just to let life happen to you.

But here's a friendly reminder: You are always responsible for creating the life you want to lead.

But to be honest, some days are harder than others.

Just as you have to guard your mind and define a career that sustains you, there's the additional opportunity to design your lifestyle.

Your home, your hairstyle, your clothing choices are tools you use to tell your story.

This chapter is all about analyzing your current choices and ensuring they communicate the story you want to tell.

QUALITY CONNECTIONS

Deep connections are the most critical part of our human existence.
Whom would I like to connect with more over the next three months?

01

02

03

04

05

06

07

08

09

10

HOME GOALS

WHAT DOES MY HOME CURRENTLY SAY ABOUT ME?

THIS IS HOW I WANT MY HOME TO FEEL...

WHAT ARE SOME SMALL CHANGES I WANT TO MAKE TO MY SPACE FOR IT TO WORK BETTER FOR ME?

WHAT SPACE WOULD I LIKE TO FOCUS ON REDECORATING OR REORGANIZING THIS QUARTER?

DEFINING ME

Circle the words from the list that best describe my personal style.

Effortless	Polished	Sleek
Comfortable	Trendy	Bohemian
Classic	Whimsical	Sultry
Quirky	Statement-Making	Understated
Experimental	Clean	Sporty
Colorful	Bold	Tailored
Elevated	Simple	Edgy
Timeless	Vintage	Downtown
Cheerful	Minimalistic	Refined
Cool	Relaxed	

USING THE WORDS ABOVE, HERE'S HOW I WOULD DEFINE MY PERSONAL STYLE.

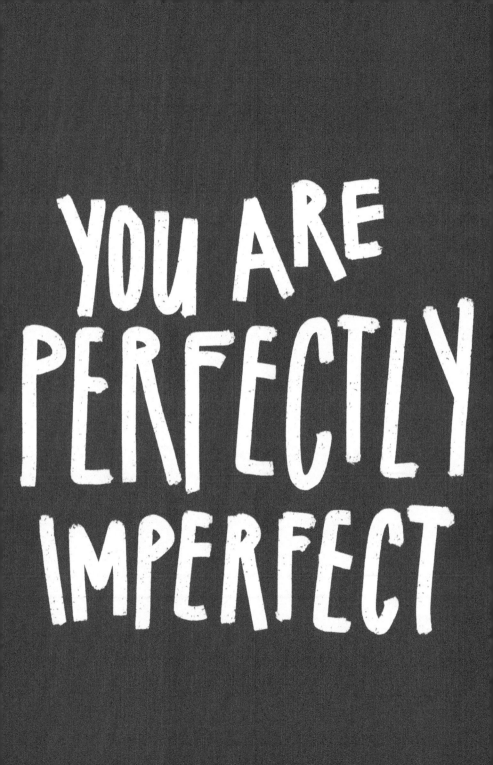

STYLE ADVICE

WHAT PIECES DO I NEED TO ADD TO MY WARDROBE?

WHO ARE MY STYLE HEROES?

WHAT'S MY FAVORITE PLACE TO SHOP? HOW WOULD I DESCRIBE THE VIBE?

WHAT SPECIFIC CLOTHING ITEMS DO I WEAR THE MOST? WHY?

WEEKEND GOALS

Here's my perfect weekend from start to finish.

TIME	ACTIVITY

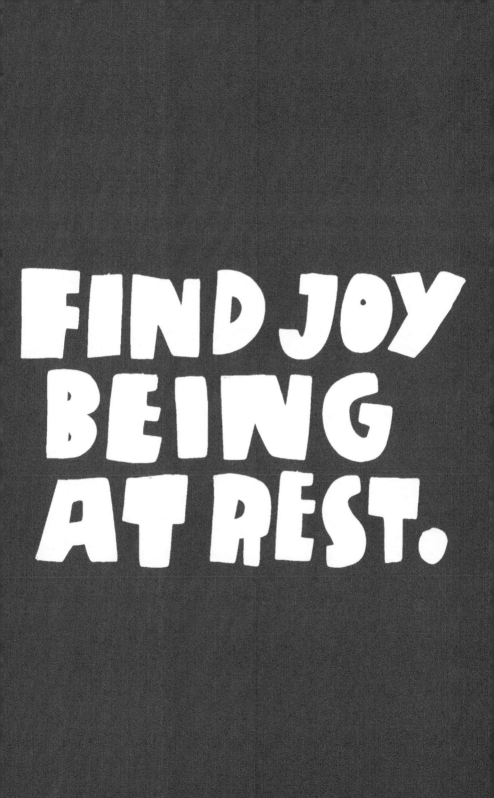

JUST FOR FUN

Life should be more than just work. List 10 things that I can do just for fun,
starting with the things I want to try in the next three months.

01

02

03

04

05

06

07

08

09

10

TRAVEL GOALS

What are five places I want to visit this year?

01

02

03

04

05

RITUALS

Creating rituals around the mundane helps give our lives more meaning.

Preparing a cup of tea and slowly savoring it while you read a magazine on a Sunday morning is a simple way to add magic to your life.

You might play a specific set of songs on the drive into work to get you pumped up for another great day.

Or burn palo santo in your studio before painting a piece of art.

These repeated actions and the symbols that they represent add a unique value to your life. They open your heart, calm your spirit, or give you the space to step outside of the everyday challenges and press a hard reset on life.

What daily, weekly, monthly, and quarterly rituals will you create?

MORNING RITUAL

My morning routine sets me up for a successful day. How do I want to
spend the first few hours of my day?

TIME	ACTIVITY

NIGHTLY RITUAL

What can I do every night to set myself up for success the next day?

TIME	ACTIVITY

DEVELOPING RITUALS

WHAT'S ONE SMALL THING I CAN DO EVERY WEEK TO CELEBRATE THAT I'M ALIVE?

ON A MONTHLY BASIS, HOW CAN I CELEBRATE MYSELF?

WHEN AM I HOLDING MY NEXT PERSONAL RETREAT? SPECIFICALLY, WHEN AND WHERE IS IT?

CHOOSE THE
ROADS THAT
LEAD TO LOVE

TINY RITUALS

WHAT IS MY RITUAL FOR CELEBRATING SMALL WINS?

WHAT IS MY RITUAL FOR WHEN I GET STRESSED OUT AT WORK?

HOW DO I CELEBRATE THE END OF A WORK WEEK?

MY PERSONAL HOLIDAYS

What is my list of set holidays I want to celebrate this year?

01

02

03

04

05

GOAL-SETTING

Real talk: The average person has way too much going on. Finding a healthy balance in work and personal life is a struggle for even the most disciplined. And honestly, we all have a little bit of procrastinator inside us.

However, there is a simple way to make deliberate action in creating good habits: Setting goals.

There's a unique and meaningful power in setting a goal, watching its headway over time, and ultimately checking it off the list. Seeing this concrete progress builds self-esteem and sets you up to take on even bigger goals.

PLANNING IS ONLY THE
FIRST STEP, THEN YOU
HAVE TO DO THE WORK

HOW TO SET AWESOME GOALS

While using The Reset Workbook, I want you to go big and bold, but I also want you to use a dash of realism. I want you to stretch yourself, but I also want you to set goals you can really accomplish in the next three months. Find those tiny wins first, and as the months progress, continue to aim bigger and brighter.

One of the most useful ways to make your goals realistic is to use the SMART framework:

S – Specific (or Significant)
M – Measurable (or Meaningful)
A – Attainable (or Action-oriented)
R – Relevant (or Rewarding)
T – Time-bound (or Trackable)

For example, you would replace "I want to eat healthier" with "I will cook three times a week using fresh ingredients." By defining your idea of success, you can easily track the goal and see if you successfully reached it.

More than that, though, you can easily develop the small first steps in getting to your bigger goals. For example, to cook three times a week, you have to start with other smaller goals:

- Research healthy recipes
- Make a shopping list
- Buy groceries
- Prep ingrdients in the morning before work
- Cook the meal

By breaking out the smaller steps in the greatest amount of detail, you can slowly start checking things off the list.

Once you start ticking tiny tasks off your list, your confidence will continue to grow to propel you closer and closer to your goals.

By continually checking in on these goals, you can also pivot whenever necessary. While goals are good guideposts, they can also frequently shift. Perhaps after two months, you realize that cooking three times a week is unrealistic for your hectic work schedule. That's totally fine.

You can always redefine your plan.

For example, maybe you retarget your focus from cooking at home to eating out at vegetarian restaurants to make sure you're eating more veggies.

MOST COMMON GOALS

Here's a list of some of the most common goals to help kickstart your brainstorming session.

Choose a healthier lifestyle

- Exercise more frequently
- Make healthier food choices
- Learn to cook
- Run a marathon
- Be more mindul
- Start journaling
- Practice yoga regularly

Start a creative hobby

- Learn to play an instrument
- Make art
- Try ceramics
- Start scrapbooking
- Create a portfolio of work

Achieve an accomplishment

- Write a novel
- Learn a new language
- Graduate from college or get a secondary degree
- Buy or build a house
- Launch a website
- Win an award
- Speak at a conference

Do something adventurous

- Go scuba diving
- Try rock climbing
- Get a tattoo
- Go bungee jumping

Practical life goals

- Get organized
- Save money
- Get a new job
- Get out of debt
- Find a romantic partner
- Plan a big vacation
- Make new friends

Personal goals

- Start a side hustle
- Get a promotion at work

BEGIN WITH THE END IN MIND

GOALS BRAINSTORM

What are some of my goals for the next three months?

01

02

03

04

05

06

07

08

09

10

NARROWING MY FOCUS

Here are the top three goals I will work on over the next three months.

01

02

03

YOU DID IT!

Your hard work deserves a pat on the back. It's no easy feat to take the time and energy to invest in building your ideal life. But you had the courage and the grit to make it happen.

I hope that this book helped you learn about yourself and the things that you want to achieve. Sit in this moment of empowerment and make your dream life a reality.

In case no one told you today: You are talented, intelligent, and capable.

You were uniquely designed to make a meaningful impact in the world. But it's your responsibility to find the strength to build the life you want to lead. That takes a daily decision to honor your future self by doing the hard work today.

I believe in you and the magic you are destined to create.

ABOUT THE AUTHOR

Justin Shiels has always been compelled by the power of words and pictures. He received his BFA in Graphic Design from Loyola University New Orleans and his Masters in Arts Administration from the University of New Orleans.

By day, he's the Creative Director at a tech company in Austin. On nights and weekends, he makes inspirational content for the internet.

He developed the workbook he always needed—something to help him design the life he wanted to live.

It was scary and hard and often made him feel like a complete fraud. But he did it because it was the work he was supposed to be doing.

What big, scary thing should you be doing right now?